DEMOLITION SUITE

DEMOLITION SUITE

poems

Willa Carroll

Split Rock Press
2023

ISBN 978-1-7354839-7-9

Cover image: Still from *Project Hazmatic*, a film by Willa Carroll.
Book layout and design by Crystal Gibbins.

Split Rock Press is dedicated to publishing eco-friendly books that explore place, environment, and the relationship between humans and the natural world.

Environmental consciousness is important to us. This book is printed with chlorine-free ink and acid-free paper stock supplied by a Forest Stewardship Council certified provider. The paper stock is made from 30% post-consumer waste recycled material.

Split Rock Press Chapbook Series readers: Amy Clark, Crystal S. Gibbins, Whitney (Walters) Jacobson, Serenity Schoonover, and Natasha Pepperl.

www.splitrockreview.org/press

TABLE OF CONTENTS

SCORE FOR THE BODY AS CAUTIONARY TALE

Sing at the feast | bowls of gravel & wire | sawdust bread | rice
carved from the moon's deciduous teeth | Wash it down | with
remediated rivers | ablated glaciers | hot blooded seas | Chase it |
with industrial slush | crude plumes | holy petroleum | Can you
hear the bells | runaway exponentials | ticking cells | Dress for
extreme weather | decked in feathers & tremors | Sun reddens at
noon | in forest fire conditions | as molecules sink into the water
table | as the field's yellow | caution tape | ribbons the wind |
After the storm | my father's hammer | craters the walls

SCORE FOR THE BODY IN TIDAL SURGE

Test the waters | crimson with algae | oil & metal ore | We long for
reasonable seasons | fires wilding | deluge on the loose | boulders
rolling home | I batten hatches for the storm | you ride the surge |
wearing the endangered | body of a bird | Wending in breadlines
we taste | germ of the grain | plague of the germ | Let the stunned
tongue say | mourning every morning | on autumn days bright with
decay | spores pixelating the wind | ants marching on empires of
weeds | mile high tides | stars wheeling across the black circuit

SCORE FOR A BODY ON THE LINE

Guard the porch | of my mouth | old spit factory | curtain the bird
of my tongue | Swaddle the moon | rename the sun | Pull milk |
from heavy fruits | from white dwarf stars | sheltering in space |
glitter harbingers | degenerate remnant planets | invisible in our
cities | Glistening targets | fragile mammals | account for your
apertures | moist portals | open to overtures | eyes issuing rivers |
Most desirable host | sheltering in place | shake that long face |
shake it shake it | like a petroleum gull | Request a fresh suit | for
human rain | chemical plumes | toxic motes | Oh don't call me |
wrecked nest

SCORE FOR THE BODY AS DEMOLITION SITE

Mind your tongue | keep an eye on the I | hiding between notes |
We play a game with no score | down on all fours | Call all ill |
animals to the yard | sweeten the debris you feed them | Jump the
electric fence | the species link | Suit up for demolition | dig
doorways into the earth | break windows into the frozen lake |
build tinder cathedrals | as sparks ride upward | We bend the night
around our shoulders | wear its heavy costume to bed | Wake to
red tidal blooms | havoc in the cells | Lend your decibels | to the
applause | your muscle for the charge | your red ochre on the walls
| your scanned fingerprints

SCORE FOR THE BODY WITH BIOACCUMULATION

Save us from cold moons | lakes of liquid methane | sunless

planets | balls with no spin | no high noon | no big crimson |

behind clouds seeded with benzene | Give us our sun | hot queen

| radiation maven | sporting a burning corona | My father lived in

the desert | between a gypsum mine | & Superstition Mountain |

He storied the last wild condors | six foot wings | their blood

spiked with DDT | I know the taste | famous poison | lacing a

generation of mother's milk | When he lost his way | under the

punishing sun | he sucked white sap from cacti | pulling spines

from his tongue

SCORE FOR COMPROMISED BODY

Ride the river | to the polyethylene sea | Trouble back upstream |
tastes of Teflon & jet fuel | forever chemicals in our blood |
Children forgive us the heavy | metals in your every | tooth & bone
| God Bless America's | contamination zones | Children drink your
polyfluoroalkyl milk | as oceans cloud over with chalky algae |
killing krill | & fish by the legion | Cousin Leviathan | swallow me
into your rank church | humid cavern of flotsam & jetsam | Teach
me your wild scores | blue fugues | drowned by engine din |
propeller roar | & offshore oil rigs

SCORE FOR THE BODY IN GEOLOGIC TIME

Report weather from the interior | extreme heat index | thunder in
the middle distance | contaminated rain & wind | We go further in
| stretching time like an accordion | as coral filters an ocean | as
kelp sways in the punctual moonlight | Shed the exoskeleton | of
sleep | as the clock glints its teeth | as four walls grow a membrane
| around the nuptial bed | Sirens begin again | as my hands find the
gills of your ribs | Wake us | first vertebrates | floating in shallow
seas | Let our fins | find dry land

SCORE FOR BODIES IN THE MIDDLE DISTANCE

Take your time | to become mammal | first membrane | to last
synapse | top predator | to big game | in a trophic cascade |
Weather the spiked crown | in hot spots | in epic centers | If we
survive the season | find me in a yellow field | or a modern canyon |
rub the velvet | from my antlers | What does the soul call the tongue
| red bridge | pet horse | wet instrument | Sing to me from a
distance | like a possessed bell | without a clapper | Let us salute as
sunflowers | salute across the crowded | room of a dream | We shed
our black confetti | we touch as seeds touch | inside the body of a
bird | Fold your animal mind | with mine | mountain to mountain

SCORE FOR A BODY ON ALL FOURS

Brace for the quake | my fault lines | my fissures issuing steam |
Hello aftershocks | boulders rolling stoned | I will blow the Big
House down | unsettling the scores | widening the antipodes |
between us | continents adrift | at far ends of the globe | Oh
molten rifts | melting poles | Sparrows steal my braille of crumbs |
I'm down on hands & knees | ducking thrown stones | drinking
from a river halfway to the sea | Ocean turning | trashed plastics |
to jagged grains | Can my hands patch the leak | in your torn floor

SCORE FOR THE BODY AS FIRE SEASON

Call me tender envelope | little tinder | rational animal | running
for the shore | Wildfires make their own weather | dry thunder |
soot snow | We shelter in a crowded burrow | under an orange
noon sky | Airlift us with Icarus wings | Calculate the weight | of
drought dust | star grit | measure loss as freight | Late now to
perform the prescribed burn | or tamp down the embers | choiring
fires | ash the place | Cue the exit music | we must flee from home
| going going | long gone with the windblown toxins | saplings
black to the root

SCORE FOR THE BODY AS CALVING GLACIER

Hold your jagged tongues | your blue sluice | I drink from your leaks | polar lobes | ablation zones | I touch your arctic bulk | friable ice | scored with cracks | I beg on my knees | halt your calving | rewind your ruptures | recall debris from risen | acidic seas | oceans swallowing coasts | Resist the sultry air | as your meltwater roves south | shifting the planetary axis | disrupting the Gulf Stream | In the deep water column | your carbon dioxide steals ions | corrodes the calcium armor of sea snails | & intricate starfish bones | Oh broken chain | begin again

SCORE FOR SOMNAMBULANT BODY

Begin in rivers | green with leached nitrogen | Begin in dirt
underfoot | Listen to the insect chorus | microbe empire | My
father sleeps in the loam | in the low clay | I'm accountable only to
the wind | & rocks shedding their skins | in acid laced rain | I lie
under a blue tarp ceiling | dreaming a modern ark | with a hole in its
hull | All morning gone | swimming in the marrow | All afternoon
spent | in the wet archive | behind the eyes | After the flood | salt
kills the pines | Out in another scorched forest | animal bones are
slow | skull a bowl | Our dust on loan | from a shapely nebula

SCORE FOR SOVEREIGN BODY

I'm not your biddable animal | handfed beast | leashed creature |
Queens mate beyond human control | high & wild | sixty feet
overhead | coupling in the upper air | with random drones | half a
score or more | Queens will be killed | at the mouth of the wrong
hive | danger at the door | We all fall | to humans or bears |
murderous hornets | toxic uptake in a flower | We all fall to viral
spikes | foulbrood surging in crowded colonies | Deploy biological
weaponry | sealing the propolis envelope around the comb | Leave
only a tiny crack | impervious to volcanic ash | as we gorge on our
store | gold cache

SCORE FOR THE BODY IN A LAND OF MILK & HONEY

Steer your makeshift raft | follow Polaris | over six troubled rivers
| seven dead seas | to bring me the last casks | of honey from a
promiscuous wilderness | All day we petition for rain | waiting out
wildfires | All night we spill the milk of human time | cupping our
hands to drink | compromised waters | fastening storms to boarded
shores | capsizing our bodies | flesh boats | mobile homes | Rend
my envelope | pluck my red hot root | our blood flooded with
legacy chemicals | Why stake your dime on us fools | top mammals
| toxic sovereigns | scorched forces | Our mighty synapses | our
fast hands | We pass like nectar | between the tongues of bees

SCORE FOR THE BODY AS TERRESTRIAL EXPERIMENT

Pledge allegiance to a dozen senses | Milk the lion | to feed the lamb | Dress the body in resin & feathers | formaldehyde & dandelion | We are a nest for the breath | sending wet motes into the wind | Measure viral load | Build a house of dirt | use a knife to score | clay slabs | add slag | fire to adhere | Call the body | ghost meat | breached sheath | spectral suit | worn by my father | his last day on earth | No solution to our porous equation | subject to chemical accumulation | Unhinge the jaws | swallow the impossible air

SCORE FOR VECTOR BODY

Call me hot target | smoldering host | caught with a machete |
whacking the bush | stealing the green patina | from unendorsed
forests | Interrogate the animals | over centuries | beginning with
the furred vermin | those excellent vectors | Then pigs & cows |
methane factories | I remain blameless | as they strafe the place |
with the Mesopotamian plague | When the next epidemic | hits
Constantinople | we blame the ships | freighted with wheat from
Egypt | cargo of fleas | riding on the backs of rats | our ancestors

SCORE FOR THE BODY AS SOFT ORACLE

We stole the omens | paid the augurs | jangled the silver | currency
cast | with the likeness of pocked monarchs | anointed with holy oil
| We burned the myrrh | tossed the salt | lit the lamps | & still
disaster visits | Blame the stars | conjunction of Saturn Jupiter Mars
| Hello Black Death | sailing the high Black Sea | We bring our
hunger | aboard to Sicily Genoa Venice | London where
enterprising girls | sing their wares in wharves | O cockles &
mussels | Centuries down the road | hazmat suited figures | bury
bodies in the loam | as gloved hands | find tar balls in the sand |
soft black coins for their eyes

SCORE FOR THE BODY WITH FRESH SPILL

Hold your fire | near the laden supertanker | metal basilica
pregnant with oil | set to leak into the Red Sea | & adolescent coral
| & old mangrove | hoarding carbon like gold | Back in the Pacific
| a fresh spill | spreads its legs | floats in sheens | surfs the
currents | roiling into ribbons | Wandering plumes | blacken the
wrack | coating the kelp | & snowy plovers | greasing their seashell
nests | Blame the anchor | pulling the pipeline like a bowstring |
Scrims & berms | sandbags stacked | in the long & short term |
cannot stop the slick

SCORE FOR THE BODY IN FEVER

No beds for the sick | check historical precedents | Boccaccio
called the bubonic | a kind of fire | in the house of the body | in
the bellowing lungs | in the warm cave of your mouth | on mine |
Requiem time | for animal appetites | Stop weeping | little pangolin
| distant cousin of the armadillo | Come kiss me in the sterile
vestibule | of a dream | Come check my PPE | my donning &
doffing rituals | In rolling hills | pocked with caves | we bed for the
night | I feel your heavy breath in mine | roving damp hands | I
feel a cleaving | in my cells | I can't catch all this wet confetti | this
spillover | over & over

SCORE FOR BODY OF TROUBLED WATER

Dive into troubled water | of a once Great Lake | where fish forage
for bright confetti | sucking down microplastics | fragments
saturated with pesticides & heavy metals | jagged edges scoring
throat & gut | Through gills | warming waters | increase chemical
uptake | Larval fathead minnows | show deformities | scoliosis |
edema around the eyes | swollen hearts & yolk sacs | truncated tails
| Centuries ago | storms sent sloops & schooners | great vessels to
the depths | Nesting in the wrecks | schools of smallmouth bass |
ribs of the hulls | hiding them like bullrush forests

SCORE FOR CLANDESTINE BODIES

Meet me behind the mountain | press me against a mineral seam | I can't sing | swallowed my tongue | when I was a bird | sick beak | greasy wings | When I see you | I nod like a bell | smile like a cracked hull | Come closer | your voice will live in the nautilus | of my ear to the wall | your pearl in my throat | I'll be the river under your floor | burning with dioxin & time | Night is a hive | we report back to | depositing toxic dew | On the bed's proscenium | we play the parts we were born for | paragon of animals | honey receptacles

SCORE FOR BODIES IN SWARM

Avoid nectar hours | high winds | or you will sweep the desiccated shells | of bees for miles | Blame the pesticide arsenal | brands named | Scorpion | Sniper | Tombstone | Warrior | Russian farmers called them | *God's little bird* | thought killing them a sin | Obey Mother Tupelo | Father Clover | I once watched one | convulsing in the pink sleeve | of a foxglove | legs twitching a sick jig | I once watched three girls | three graces at Coney Island | pouring jars of honey over their heads | then beer | then more honey | making mead of themselves | then rushing into the waves | crying *miel miel*

SCORE FOR THE BODY BETWEEN SEED & THORN

A flower is a series of events in time | & the origin of the apple |
the orange | the lemon | dimpled skin | shining with fungicide |
Rain consorts with the trees | I need a machine made of sound |
soft detonations | scores for the body to perform | I put my ear to
the wall | of your chest | for the flesh drum | Cell by cell | you
remake yourself | We are both bee & comb | Good world |
surrender your nectar | kick pollen into the wind | deconstruct the
bud | blowing it open | Between seed & thorn | satin & rot | we
take what you've got | all the sweet debris | every last bird

SCORE FOR REACTOR BODY

Conduct a bird report | an insect census | Note the voles |
devouring radioactive mushrooms | see the opals of their eyes |
cataract moons | Note the albino barn swallows | the absent
cuckoos | We followed the fallout | to reindeer in Norway | their
meat delicious with lingonberries | American honey still tells | of
detonations | cesium in the nectar | Fukushima spiders surprise us
| numbers rising with radiation | A wildlife camera in Chernobyl |
captures the faces of two boars | nine badgers | twenty-six gray
wolves | sixty raccoon dogs | ten red foxes | No more two headed
calves | though isotopes froth the milk | The morning of the
disaster | bees elected | to stay silent in their hives | *A bad omen* |
said one farmer's wife

SCORE FOR THE BODY AS CHEMICAL BOND

Pull her from the shale | our sister Ethane | Drag her to that
massive factory | perched on the Gulf Coast | pelican heaven |
petrochemical hell | jumping with mullet | shrimp bobbing like
question marks | in polyester nets | Get her so hot | superheated to
crack her gas | break her bonds | her molecular bones | out of
which will spring | her daughter Ethylene | ruler of a plastic
kingdom | Queen of adhesives & resins | Root monarch | of
crushed plastic bottles | & pharmaceutical chemicals | Taste her
oxide in the hothouse air | taste her degrading in water | traces of
her found in our bowels | in our blood's retort

SCORE FOR BODIES IN APPEAL

Give us a chemical halo | a non-stick life | in control of the
elements | Conquer water with Gore-Tex | Meet flame with Teflon
| no charred marrow | no greased adhesions | Scotchgard keeps us
watertight | bone dry eyes | boots like citadels | molecules heckling
| blood levels | for miles around | Map the plumes | compromised
soil | beneath the skin of the mountain | Track the particulate wind
| back to the factory | of high performance materials | In a town
called Hoosick Falls | we ride the lubricated river | froth at the
mouth | of troubled watersheds | My face an appeal | at the
bottom of the well

SCORE FOR THE BODY POLITIC

Uranium climbs the bones | of children | ruckusing near
abandoned mines | small bodies scaling | heaps of tailings | On
Navajo land | Diné territory | trucks lug toxic rock | as radioactive
grit | sloughs into the wind | blows towards homes | Underground
seams | & abandoned shafts | leak downstream | leaching
radionuclides | into groundwater | wrecking the wells | Find the
holders | who called the mines | mine | Rattle the chain of custody
| Target the end users | bomb makers | war hawks | Indict
responsible parties | governing bodies | Our body politic | standing
by | as my father swallows dust clouds | cuts pipes fleshed with
asbestos | same killer mineral | lining the bellies of warships

SCORE FOR REWILDING BODY

Invite the lichen | to colonize the rocks | dress up the deserts |
tamp down the dust storms | Summon the moss | to hold the soil
| microbe circus underfoot | Enlist fungi | to sop up oil | spilled in
the brownfield lot | Big bad wolves | make your comeback |
rewind trophic cascades | revive the wild | culling elk | Save shrubs
for mice & bison | devoured by owls & mountain lions | Spare
willow | for beavers in winter | governing rivers | Recruit otters |
their pelts once called | soft gold

SCORE FOR THE BODY AS LAST FRONTIER

Poachers prize the rosette pelt | bones are gold | on the black
market | I put on the body | of this snow leopard | my eyes behind
hers | scanning terrain | We pant across borders | Russia Mongolia
China Tibet | Plush paws | doing twenty five miles a night | boreal
forest to tundra to Himalayas | Preying on blue sheep in Nepal |
not really blue | Sleeping on straw | dying of a virus | in a
Nebraskan zoo | They say a glacier losing girth | has no income |
permafrost spent too soon | Trickling muck | replaces the
headwaters | Mekong Yangtze Yellow | rivers without mouths |
never to taste the sea

SCORE FOR BODIES DRESSED IN POLLEN

Dress in pollen | dance in code | Stay loyal to one or two flowers |
Follow the pigment | my red specialist | my blue connoisseur |
Build your hive in an abandoned tire | rolling down the road | Here
comes my father around the bend | of a dream | wearing a crown of
bees | sawdust on his shoes | In winter we filled our pockets | with
black seeds | waited in a grove | hands outstretched for chickadees |
dark caps matching | the hulls in their beaks | Sunflowers are said |
to pull radiation from the soil | In the fields near Fukushima |
shaggy coronas | beaded faces | Around Chernobyl | gold sentinels

SCORE FOR THE BODY AS TIME MACHINE

Rewind the sun | set back the burning clock | sweep debris into a
moon | score a cluster of stars | Reenact plate tectonics | great
oxygenations | Swim trilobite swim | as flowers precede the bees |
as whales flunk back into the oceans | Mountains trending up | seas
retreat | glaciers advance | We invent the kiss | record an inch of
history | grease wheels | melt poles | Volcanoes wear down to nubs
| buildings to braille | Nuclear waste | takes the time it takes |
along with coral revival | & continental rifts | Decamp with the
moon | in galactic drift | Dial down the sun | red giant | white
dwarf | runaway star

ACKNOWLEDGMENTS

TriQuarterly published "Project Hazmatic," a video piece incorporating earlier versions of these poems in its soundtrack. This project won Best Poetry Film at the International Migration & Environmental Film Festival and has screened at several international film festivals. Earlier versions of these poems appeared in *About Place Journal, DMQ Review, Global Poemic, Heavy Feather Review, Interim Poetics, Rogue Agent, Surviving Corona Crisis, The Dodge, Under a Warm Green Linden, What Rough Beast,* and *Wild Roof Journal.* An earlier version of this chapbook was a finalist for the Tomaž Šalamun Prize. Three poems were finalists for the Regeneration Literary Contest at *Ninth Letter.*

ABOUT THE AUTHOR

Willa Carroll is a writer and interdisciplinary artist. Her debut full-length poetry collection, *Nerve Chorus* (The Word Works), was noted in *The Common* as a "meticulously choreographed treatment of life as art." Carroll's poems have appeared in *AGNI, Poem-A-Day, Tin House, The Slowdown,* and elsewhere. A finalist for The Georgia Poetry Prize and the Tomaž Šalamun Prize, she won *Narrative Magazine's* Third Annual Poetry Contest and *Tupelo Quarterly's* TQ7 Poetry Prize, judged by Brenda Hillman. Her poetry videos and multimedia collaborations have been featured in *Interim Poetics, Narrative Outloud,* and *TriQuarterly.* Awarded Best Poetry Film at the International Migration and Environment Film Festival, her work has screened at festivals in the US, Canada, UK, and Denmark. After earning degrees from Bennington and living in NYC for twenty-five years, she's now based in upstate New York. willacarroll.com

Made in the USA
Monee, IL
29 October 2023

45351659R00023